THE
ABC's
OF
ASSURANCE

by

John H. Gerstner, Ph.D.

Soli Deo Gloria Publications
...for instruction in righteousness...

Soli Deo Gloria Publications
P. O. Box 451, Morgan, PA 15064
(412) 221-1901/FAX 221-1902

*

The ABC's of Assurance is © 1991
by John H. Gerstner.

*

ISBN 1-877611-39-5

*

Second Printing 1998

Dedication

To Harry Ament, who built the study in which this little book was written. We do different work, but for the same Lord Jesus Christ. And we both love Him - with all our heart.

TABLE OF CONTENTS

TABLE OF CONTENTS

The A B C's of Assurance

"Blessed Assurance, Jesus is Mine." If I know that Jesus is mine, I cannot have anything but a blessed assurance for ever and ever. If all I can say is, "Jesus is mine for the moment," I have a blasted assurance. I hope that the reader who knows that Jesus is his/hers for the moment, finds that that moment is a moment that lasts forever and ever. *This is life eternal, that they know Thee, the only true God and Jesus Christ whom He has sent* (John 17:3).

This little book tries to cover the big topics on this theme: propounding arguments for, answering arguments against, and weighing them all in the divine scales of Holy Scripture. There are twenty-six articles here, one for each letter of the alphabet. There are fifty-two Sundays in a year, which means one of the fifty-two <u>ABC's of Assurance</u> could, if you wished for study and meditation purposes, be read every other Sabbath.

I must forewarn the reader. Some of these ABC's are simple and obvious. Others involve complexities. Some are polemical. Remember, most Christians do <u>not</u> have or believe that they <u>should have</u> assurance of eternal salvation. <s>Your author believes that Christians can have, ought to have, must have, assurance.</s> It is a duty, to be sure. If you ponder these meditations carefully, I hope you are Christians and that you know it assuredly.

All of our topics deal with assurance, concentrating on one text especially, but not exclusively. Some seem clearly favoring assurance. Others are constantly appealed to against the doctrine. There is no order of treatment, except the alphabetical. This is not the best way to <u>study</u> a doctrine, but it has its advantages. One advantage is the timing and regularity. The other is that the points meet us at random as they do in life, but not in the classroom. Third, it keeps us constantly aware of how the 9/10ths think and live. Finally, it keeps us examining our spiritual pulses.

<u>It is a shame for true Christians not to have assurance. It is a crime for non-Christians to have assurance.</u>

John H. Gerstner
Ligonier, PA 15658

Assurance of Eternal Salvation

Now this is eternal life, that they may know Thee, the only true God, and Jesus Christ, whom Thou hast sent. (John 17:3)

Assurance of salvation is not really our topic. It is assurance of eternal salvation. A person may have assurance of his present salvation, but believe that he could lose his salvation tomorrow. He certainly doesn't have assurance of eternal salvation, then. There is a basic difference between these two conceptions. A person may believe that he is in Christ Jesus now. Tomorrow morning he could wake up dead in trespasses and sins. That fact makes him unsure today. Tomorrow's uncertainty takes away today's certainty.

The assurance of salvation that we are talking about in this book is what is usually meant by the doctrine. That is, a person is not only sure of his present salvation but, on the basis of that present assurance, he is sure that he will have eternal salvation. You can see that that would rest on the notion that he cannot fall from grace. If he believed that he could fall from grace, assurance of eternal salvation would fall with it.

Temporary assurance is no assurance at all.
A theology that allows for a fall from grace
simply does not allow for assurance of no fall
from grace. This is all by way of showing
what is meant by assurance AND WHAT IS
NOT MEANT. Remember, the greatest and
most vital, personal question a Christian can
ever ask himself is, "Do I have assurance of
eternal life?"

Christ, in John 17:3, shows that true knowledge of God and His Son is eternal life. If you
truly know Him now, you truly possess Him
- forever!

Other Scriptures teach us to have assurance
of understanding (Colossians 2:2), of faith
(Hebrews 10:22), and of hope (Hebrews 6:11).
These texts do not tell Christians that they
possess assurance, but only their duty to
possess it. John 17:2 teaches us that, if we
savingly know God, we have God forever.
That is not merely duty; that is experience.
Still some Christians deny the undeniable.

IF THERE IS NO TOMORROW,
THERE IS NO TODAY.

Beating the Body

Paul writes in I Corinthians 9:26-27, ...*I do not fight like a man beating the air.* <u>*No, I beat*</u> <u>*my body and make it my slave so that after I*</u> <u>*have preached to others, I myself will not be*</u> <u>*disqualified for the prize.*</u>

This passage tells us two things. <u>First, Paul,</u> <u>the Christian apostle, was a severely self-dis-</u> <u>ciplined person.</u> *I beat my body* must mean that he kept its desires in subjection ("my slave") to his will. This was not easy. He had to fight and keep fighting. More than fight, <u>he had to win</u> the fight. <u>He couldn't beat the</u> <u>air. He had to beat his flesh.</u> *not literally*

Today, many people who think themselves Christians and are church members don't even beat the air. They have given up the fight. <u>There is no fight left in them. They jus-</u> <u>tify the flesh's victory.</u> When I was young, fornication was considered <u>by the world</u> "sowing one's wild oats" for a period until a guy settled down with a wife and had a family. Today, our culture doesn't make you settle down <u>before or after</u> you have a wife and family. What was once considered a light sin for a short period is now (though far grosser) no sin at all, but a style for life.

This leads us to our second point. Paul testified that if he did not win his battle against the body, he would be damned. He might have sinfully continued to preach to men, but he would be rejected by God. He would be a person <u>saving others by the gospel while damning himself</u> in so doing. Many modern "Christians" are committing overt fornication, adultery, homosexuality, all kinds of perversion, still thinking themselves acceptable to a God who insists that He will not be mocked. But whatever a man sows, that he will reap. The modern licentiate gets his reward only in this world where others, perverted in judgment if not in lifestyle, may praise him. When he comes to the next world, he will pay his dues to God, for whom "the wages of sin is (eternal) death."

Some of those who abhor such contemporary wickedness and shun such immorality themselves, nevertheless commit the sin of misinterpreting the Word of God. They honor Paul for beating his body, but then attribute serious error to him!

How so? Some conservatives say that Paul would be rejected or disqualified as an apostle or minister, but not damned to hell. "He would," they say, "be put on the shelf." But Jesus Christ thinks differently. *I tell you the truth, everyone who sins* (beats the air rather than his flesh) *is a slave to sin* and Satan (John 8:34f.), which puts a person in hell, not on any shelf.

The question concerning assurance still remains. Is Paul, the Arminian evangelical will ask, not admitting that he could be lost? If even an apostle could fall and go to hell, he and no one else can be legitimately sure of eternal life! ~~The Apostle Paul never said that he might have fallen and gone to hell. He said that if (instead of making his body his slave he allowed himself to become its slave), he certainly would go to hell.~~

But he did not say that he would or could become the slave of his body. He said only that if he did, he would be rejected by God. Even Jesus Christ said that if He said He did not know God, He would be a liar! *Though you do not know Him* (God), *I know Him. If I said I did not, I would be a liar like you...* (John 8:55). No Christian would ever imagine that the Son of God could have become a liar. But He, Himself, said that IF He denied that He knew God, <u>He would be a liar</u>!

Every Christian must say the same thing. <u>If</u> he gives himself over to lust or lying or any other sin, he will be damned because he thereby proves Himself <u>not</u> to be a Christian. A true Christian is no more capable of doing that than Paul was capable of becoming a sex-addict or Jesus Christ a liar.

> A CHRISTIAN BEATS HIS BODY
> TILL THE LUST OR LAZINESS
> IS DRIVEN OUT OF IT.

Captain of Our Salvation

For it became Him, for whom <u>are</u> all things and by who <u>are</u> all things in bringing many sons unto glory, to make the captain of their salvation perfect through sufferings.
(Hebrews 2:6)

Christ is sometimes called the Author rather than the Captain of our salvation. I prefer to think that *archegos* translates better as "captain" here. If one renders it "author," please remember that Christ is not only Author, but also Finisher, of our salvation (Hebrews 12:2). In that sense, "Captain," as well as "Author and Finisher," include what I wish to stress here.

In syllogistic form, the argument goes:

> 1. Christ is sure of victory.
> 2. Christ is the Captain of His army of disciples.
> 3. So Christ's army can be sure of victory.

If, as W.E. Henly imagined,

"I am the master of my fate,
I am the captain of my soul,"

I could have an absolute assurance of my
damnation. If Jesus Christ is the "Captain of
my soul," I can have an absolute assurance of
my salvation.

It is <u>blasphemy</u> to think a man can save himself. It is <u>blasphemy not</u> to think that Christ
can, without possibility of failure, save him.

Rudolf Bultmann once asked the question:
Does Christ save me because He is God, or is
Christ God because He saves me? The fa-
mous existentialist gave the wrong answer,
of course. No, it is only because Christ is God
that He can save - and cannot fail.

If I am my own captain, I can never succeed.
If someone other than Jesus Christ is my captain, he could not achieve the goal if he
would, and he would not if he could. But
Captain Jesus can and will. Who can doubt
that? Where would any uncertainty arise?
What can be surer than sure?

If I am not sure of my Captain, that would
only be because I am not sure that He is my

Captain. But if I am sure that Christ is the Captain of my salvation, I must be sure of my salvation.

If there was not one other word in all of Scripture on our theme than the simple statement that Jesus Christ is the Captain of His people, assurance of eternal salvation is absolutely certain.

No ENEMIES (WITHIN OR WITHOUT) CAN STAND AGAINST CAPTAIN JESUS.

Disciples are Defined as Those who Persevere in Christ's Teaching

If you hold to My teaching, you are really My disciples. (John 8:31)

This is the closest-grained argument for assurance of salvation in this whole book. This text defines a disciple as one who holds to Christ's teaching. Such a person, and only such a person, meets the very <u>definition</u> of a Christian. If one <u>does not abide</u> in His Word, that person is simply not a disciple.

If a person fails to persevere, he does not fail to be a disciple. You can't drop out of this school because, if you did, you would thereby prove that you never enrolled.

<u>IF YOU LOSE IT,
YOU NEVER HAD IT.</u>

It is said of Demas that he had forsaken the apostolic company. But, in Christ's doctrine, that means that he never joined it. *They went out from us, but they were not of us.* (I John 2:19)

People should realize they should never say that they do not believe in the perseverance of the saints. Unless, of course, they mean to say that they do not believe in Jesus Christ and never did. Because one who does not continue to believe in Jesus Christ never did believe in Him - never was a saint. It is ironical that the "Disciples of Christ" believe they can cease to believe in Christ. In that case, they are not Disciples of Christ, since Christ says that those who do not continue are not disciples and never have been! You cannot be a disciple of Christ unless you abide in Him. The proper title should not be "Disciples of Christ," but "Disciples (at least some of us, maybe) of Christ."

How does this word "disciple" bear on assurance? So closely that disciple and assured person are identical. It is not enough to believe in perseverance to be a disciple, as Christ defines disciple. You must believe assuredly that you will abide in His Word, or you have no right to call yourself a disciple. So assurance of salvation is a part of being saved. Salvation and assurance appear to be inseparable. You can't be Christ's without being a disciple, and you can't be a disciple without being one who is incapable of falling and knows it (assuredly)!

Unless, of course, you are ignorant of the Bible or wrongly instructed? Yes and no. Yes, at the moment of conversion you may not be aware of this Bible doctrine. That need can be quickly met. If you are the victim of false teaching, more time and struggling may be necessary. Where are you in the meantime? Unassured? No, living in Christ and knowing (sensing) that this is forever. You really have assurance and don't "know" it. Like a baby, you are alive and going on living indefinitely. You are aware of that but you have to grow into understanding (realization) of it.

DISCIPLESHIP IS FOREVER - OR NEVER.

Endure to the End to be Saved

But he that shall endure to the end, the same shall be saved. (Matthew 24:13)

To the Arminian evangelical mind, this is one of the great <u>anti</u>-assurance texts of the Bible. To any mind, at first glance, it is totally against assurance of salvation <u>before death</u>. It says to most people, it's not over 'till it's over. The thief-on-the-cross could be saved at the last moment, and any Christian could be lost at the last moment. You can't be sure about eternal life until you're in heaven.

Did Christ say that one can't be sure until he endures to the end? No, you admit. He did not say that. But He did say that only those are saved who do endure to the end. That is correct. But that is <u>not</u> the same thing as saying no one can know before the end that he will endure to the end and be saved.

We cited (in chapter "B") Christ's words about Himself. If He said He did not know God, He would be a liar. Would He have to wait till the end before He knows He will not become a liar? He knew and you know He would never sin in this world. Conceivably, other persons could know they would endure to the end.

But, you say, they are not God. I remind you that Paul was not God either. Yet he knew before he had endured to the end of life that he would endure (2 Timothy 4:8). So, though it is true that saved ones endure to the end, and those who endure to the end are saved ones, there is nothing to prevent them from knowing assuredly that they will endure to the end before they have endured to the end. What is impossible with men is possible (and certain) with God in men.

One is reminded in this connection that one who puts his hand to the plow and turns back is not worthy to be Christ's disciple (Luke 9:62). That is the description of a man who did not endure to the end, and manifestly was not saved. Nor could he have known before the end that he would endure to the end.

The Arminian evangelical who puts his hand to the plow cannot, on his principles, know that he will endure to the end of the first furrow. But, as I have shown elsewhere, he cannot even know, on his principles, that he has put his hand to the plow.

To put it briefly: (1) Only those who endure to the end will be saved. (2) That truth does not imply that no one can <u>know</u> before the end that he will endure to the end. (3) Therefore, the text is no argument against assurance of eternal life here and now, <u>before</u> journey's end.

THOSE ENDURING NOW ARE
ENDURING TO THE END.

Free-Will Makes Assurance Impossible

He came to that which was His own, but His own did not receive Him. Yet to all who received Him, to those who believed in His name, He gave the right to become children of God. (John 1:11-12)

I have a former student and friend who has been in classes of mine from time to time. He is a professor himself, and he teaches non-assurance to his students. Nevertheless, he claims to have assurance! Every time we meet, he assures me that he has assurance. Nevertheless, he believes that he could fall from grace at any moment. When I say to him, "How can you have assurance of salvation when you believe you can fall from grace at any moment? The only kind of assurance that you can have is that at this moment you are saved, and you can't even be sure of that!" I don't remind him that there would be a strong temptation for a person who believed that he certainly had salvation now but might not have it the next minute to think of some way of terminating his life! He could feel sure at the present moment, but that could change any moment.

You say, it would be a fall from grace itself if a person deliberately committed suicide. That would show he was not a believer. Suicide would be a good way of taking yourself out of the salvation you are now assured of. I try to explain to my friend that he ought to recognize that fact. His theological convictions rule out the state of mind in which he finds himself. If he has real assurance of salvation, then he will have to give up his theology, which teaches that he is able to fall out of grace. If he does believe that he can fall out of grace any moment, then he ought to give up his personal claim.

Nevertheless, every time I meet him he has been in a state of assurance. He is quite aware of the fact that the doctrine he is relying on means once in a state of grace, always in a state of grace. But he is as sure that that doctrine is wrong as that his experience is right! But he has no right at all to assurance of salvation. That doesn't stop him. He still insists he has the same type of assurance of salvation that I do who has a doctrinal foundation for such assurance.

My friend tries to defend his inconsistent position by an analogy. He says, "I love my wife now, and I know I'll love her as long as she lives. I know I love Jesus Christ more than I love my wife and I know now that I always will love Him." I remind him at that point "You are contradicting yourself when you say 'I know now that I always will love Jesus Christ.' According to your theology, you know now that you may <u>not</u> always love Jesus Christ. You can be sure of your continuing love for your wife but, according to your own theology, you cannot be sure of your continuing love for Jesus Christ." But though we have had several conversations to this effect it never reaches him. He is a living contradiction. His heart is at war with his mind. He claims an assurance that he has now and will never lose, though, according to his doctrine, he may lose it in the time it takes to say that he cannot.

Our text above is constantly cited by opponents of assurance to show that some do <u>not</u> believe and some do. Some <u>will to believe</u> and some will <u>not to believe</u>. Ironically, the rest of the text says that those who willed to believe were *children born not of natural descent, nor of human decision or a husband's will, but born of God*. So, though some men do "will" to come to Christ, it is only those who were "born of God." In the day of the Lord's power (not the will's power), the people will be willing (Psalm 110:3).

"FREE-WILL" SPELLS BONDAGE FOREVER.

God's Golden Unbreakable Chain

For those God foreknew, He also predestined to become conformed to the image of His Son, that He might be the firstborn among many brothers. And those He predestined, He also called; those He called, He also justified; those He justified, He also glorified. (Romans 8:29-30)

Here is the divine, unbreakable chain:

1. Foreknew (or foreloved)
2. Predestined
3. Conformed
4. Called
5. Justified
6. Glorified

This chain reaches from eternity to eternity. Those who are part of it are in the mind and heart of the eternal "I AM" as long as He is, and will be with Him as long as the eternal "I AM" continues to be. We sometimes hear of security "from womb to tomb." That is less than a second in comparison of security from eternity to eternity.

If a person is part of this chain, nothing less than assurance of eternal salvation is imaginable. If you can fall, God can fall. If you can fail, God can fail. If you do not arrive, God has not arrived. DENYING CERTAINTY IS DENYING GOD! If you are not sure of your salvation, you are not sure of God. If God has foreloved you, He has glorified you. If you question your glorification, you question His Deity. You would have to be a virtual atheist to doubt your glorification. *He who believes in Me has eternal life and never dies.*

Really, the chain is not even a chain of links. It is a solid, golden bar. All its many links are molded into one way, one highway to heaven.

The reason our text breaks the golden highway into many parts is because we cannot think as God thinks - instantly, perfectly, in one eternal intuition. We must plod step by step, from link to link. Even among us, some understand much more quickly and wholistically. That is the reason God gives human teachers to His people, to guide the sheep and carry the lambs. Those who believe are on

God's highway, which has no detours and always reaches its destination. God has put us on that highway, keeps us on that highway, and will not let us leave that highway! If we could stray, we would. If He will keep us, we will not. We are sure of one thing or the other. If He lets us go, we can be sure we will end up lost. If He will not let us go, we are sure that we cannot be lost. AND GOD WILL NEVER LET US GO!

Arminians also reject "God's Golden Chain" in favor of man's "Brazen" chain.

ETERNAL LOVE THAT
WILL NOT LET ME GO.

He Who Began a Good Work

...being confident of this, that he who began a good work in you will carry it on to completion until the day of Christ Jesus....
(Philippians 1:6)

The question with a text like this is, How could there be any difference of opinion about its meaning? It seems so obvious that it says that Christians should:

1. Be confident or assured about eternal salvation.

2. Because He (God) began this good, saving work in you (the implication being that God would never begin anything He did not intend to complete).

3. But we are not left to mere implication, for the text says that God will "carry it on to completion."

4. And carrying on a good work to completion would have to mean to perfect sanctification from which one could never fall.

5. Finally, "completion" is identified with

"until the day of Christ Jesus," which must mean the day of His return and judgment, when saints "inherit the kingdom prepared for you" (heaven) from which none ever fall.

6. So Christians are assured absolutely that they have a work of God which will be brought through this world of sin and shame to completion and perfection in heaven. What could be more assuring, and how can any Christian <u>not</u> have assurance on the basis of Philippians 1:6?

However, we know that almost all Bible believers who read this text find no basis for assurance in it. How can they <u>not</u> find assurance and have assurance if they believe (as they do) that Christ is now in their hearts? Can God fail? Could the Word of God err? How can Arminians not see the obvious?

Let's see how they do it. It's really very simple. They simply deny that God does begin or carry on the good work of salvation. The Christian - not Christ - begins, carries on, and completes his salvation.

Thank God, such persons have no assurance.

of eternal salvation on these principles. There can't be any salvation - much less assurance - because man never begins, much less finishes, salvation.

Let me explain. Arminian evangelicals believe that Jesus provides salvation, but the fallen sinner begins it in himself by his faith. But, until a sinner is born again by God, he never will believe. So any "faith" produced by the sinner is a work of the flesh and not true saving faith at all. Likewise, a sinner never completes salvation of himself because it is only as God works in him "to will and to do" that he works out to completion real salvation. On evangelical principles of self-salvation, by using the grace Christ provides, there can never be any momentary salvation, much less eternal salvation.

"Jesus saves" means Jesus provides and applies salvation, and that, and only that, means assured eternal salvation.

WE ARE SURE BECAUSE WE DO NOT BEGIN OR FINISH OUR SALVATION - **GOD DOES**!

I Know Whom I Have Believed

I know whom I have believed, and am convinced that He is able to guard what I have entrusted to Him for that day. (II Tim. 1:12)

1. A Christian is one who knows Jesus Christ.

2. A Christian is one who trusts Jesus Christ for his eternal salvation.

3. A Christian is one who trusts Jesus Christ alone and entirely for his salvation.

4. Jesus Christ is the One who promises to save all who put their trust in Him for their eternal salvation.

5. Jesus Christ is One who turns away no one who comes to Him for eternal salvation.

6. Jesus Christ is infinitely trustworthy in His promises.

7. Jesus Christ is infinitely able to perform His promises.

8. Question: Where, O where, can any uncertainty of eternal life come in for any who believe?

9. Question: Where, O where, can there be room for anything but absolute assurance of eternal salvation?

10. Conclusion: Only those can be uncertain of eternal salvation who do not believe Jesus Christ is trustworthy OR do not trust themselves to Jesus Christ for eternal salvation.

I KNOW HIM MEANS, "I HAVE
ASSURANCE OF ETERNAL SALVATION."

Judas Iscariot's Apostasy
(And Israel's)

I tell you the truth, one of you is going to be-tray Me. (John 13:21)

Jesus Christ chose Judas Iscariot to be one of His apostles when He knew that Judas was an apostate unbeliever. Our explanation is this: Jesus was a true man, and he under-went some experiences as a man, not in His divine nature. Thus He ate, though as God He never became hungry and had no teeth or mouth to chew and digest food. Christ also slept, though as God He neither slumbers nor sleeps.

As an example for His people, and for His fel-low-ministers of the Word, He proceeded as they do, utilizing only His natural human powers (which do not include omniscience). He chose Judas Iscariot (just as He chose the other eleven apostles) on the basis of his pro-fession and his known behavior. On those tests, all twelve apostles proved to be suit-able. Of the twelve, one was a deceiver. He pretended to believe what he didn't believe and he pretended to be living the life he was not living.

That is exactly the same kind of "mistake" that a faithful ministerial servant of Jesus Christ can make when he passes favorably on receiving someone into the membership or even officer-ship in the Christian church. He is restricted to his finite capacities, which do not include the ability to discern the thoughts and intents of the heart and, in many cases, even to know the outward behavior of persons completely.

In a way, Christ is comforting His ministers, who "fail" in the process of doing their duty faithfully and as competently as they are capable. As a minister myself, that is a consolation to me. The fact that I have and do fail in various judgments is not necessarily traceable to carelessness on my own part. I may have examined a person quite thoroughly and, on the basis of all the information which I had, made a correct judgment which turned out to be an incorrect judgment. That particular "mistake" was indeed no real mistake. I did my duty in that particular case and made a correct judgment on the basis of the available information. *Jesus did not make a mistake in this.*

Someone may not be very comfortable with this and may say, "I don't deny that that seems to be a possibility. I do admit that our Lord Himself says that He was ignorant about certain things which He certainly was not ignorant about as far as His deity was concerned. He could have been justifiably ignorant about the state of Judas' heart as far as His human nature was concerned and it be no reflection whatever on His divine omniscience. But where does that leave us?"

Jesus knew (what people thought.)

I would say it leaves us with the possibility of Jesus doing exactly what some say He could not possibly have done. He could have made a "mistake" that was no real mistake. It was no reflection on His omniscience or His deity. He was simply acting *qua* man and not *qua* God. Then we can grant that Jesus Christ did, as God, know the state of Judas' heart, but, as man, did not know it.

What does all of this have to do with assurance of salvation? It has everything to do with it. We have no proof at all that Judas Iscariot ever was a true Christian. We have no proof at all that he fell from grace. He must have been a <u>professed</u> converted believer. Nothing more is certain. Unless it can be shown that he was once a believer, nothing has been proven against the doctrine of assurance of salvation by his apostasy and suicide.

The same is true with the nation of Old Testament Israel. For nearly two thousand years, now, it has been a rejected <u>people</u> of God (though not all individuals). If it could have been said, as Amos does, *you only, of all the families of the earth have I known,* surely the Jewish people are no longer that. Jesus Christ said, *salvation is of the Jews,* and later rejected those very Jews. *He came unto His own and His own received Him not,* and He Himself received them not (Cf. the Parable of the Vineyard, Matthew 21:33ff.). Whatever possible future the Jews may have, for the last two thousand years they have not been, as a people, the people of God. Do we have here a national fall from grace? If so, that would be the mother of arguments against assurance of salvation!

The Apostle Paul has addressed this question specifically in the eleventh chapter of his epistle to the Romans. He asks the question, *Has God rejected Israel?* He had chosen

Israel and He was rejecting Israel at the time He was choosing the Gentiles for His people, who were then grafted into the original olive tree from which the natural branches (Israel) had been cut off. Paul makes it very clear that God had not rejected Israel, for *the calling and election of God are without repentance.* The Apostle explains that God never called all Israel to eternal salvation, but only some within Israel (such as the 7,000 who had not bowed the knee to Baal, and Paul himself). The principle was that not all are Israel who are in Israel, Romans 9:6.

The true Israelites were chosen to eternal life and not one of them was, or ever will be, lost. They can be sure of that! So, *all (true) Israel will be saved.* (Romans 11:25)

JUDAS NEVER WAS A TRUE OFFICER OF CHRIST, THOUGH CHOSEN BY CHRIST.

Knowing How You are in a State of Grace

I know whom I have believed. (IITim. 3:9)

How does a person know that he has eternal life? How does he know that he is in a state of grace, even if he does know that <u>if</u> he is in a state of grace he will remain so forever? That is the practical question of greatest importance to those who are assured of the doctrine of assurance. Granted, if it is true that if I am in such a state, I will be so forever; but how do I know I am in such a state?

First of all, one must examine his heart. *For who among man knows the thoughts of a man except the man's spirit within him?* (I Corinthians 2:11). We know that we can know ourselves and our motivations. Inspired Scripture confirms our opinion in that regard; a man knows the things of man. He cannot know the things of God, Paul reminds us, unless God tells us the things that are in <u>His</u> heart. We can know what is in our own heart.

Nevertheless, because he is fallen, man is prone to self-esteem, and to think more highly of himself than he ought to think. Especially is this true in the realm of salvation and eternal destiny.

What do you find (as you examine your life carefully) to be the case? Do you love Jesus Christ? Do you believe and accept gladly the Word of God? Do you love your enemies, as well as your friends? Do you deny yourself? Do you take up your cross and follow Him? Are you evil-spoken of by an evil world, inasmuch as no one can live godly in Christ Jesus and not suffer persecution? Are you suffering persecution? There are literally thousands of questions like that, and you don't have to sit down and figure out what they are because they are raised in your experience almost everyday of your life. When you are called upon, for example, to choose one thing or another, what determines your choice? Is it a desire to honor and glorify God, or simply to appeal to your own preferences? Never a day goes by without evil being sufficient for it. You must examine yourselves to see whether that evil finds a friend or an enemy in you.

Even in this area of examination, one has to proceed with fear and trembling. I know some persons who have no assurance of their salvation because they recognize, on self-examination, that they are not perfect. They remember that they have spoken evilly of somebody, or they have lied in a given situation, or they have committed adultery, or fornication, or have broken the Sabbath day. A number of things <u>could lead</u> a person to doubt his salvation entirely, but <u>not be a ground</u> for denying his salvation. The Bible teaches that those who are entitled to an assurance of salvation are not perfect. They sin in thought, word, and deed daily, as the Catechism says. <u>Not</u> loving God, or your neighbor, or yourself, with <u>all</u> your heart, soul, mind, and strength, is a part of Christian imperfection. That does <u>not</u> prove that you are unconverted and unentitled to assurance, however.

If you ask the question, "Well, then, how does a person know on the basis of self-examination, whether he is in a state of grace or not? You say that he could have sinned, and continued in sin in the matter of inadequate love for God, man, and self, and that he could have committed fornication or lying or a dozen other sins in his lifetime, and yet you say that does <u>not</u> prove that he is an unconverted person, not in a state of grace.

What <u>does</u> prove it?"

Scripture says on this matter that sins of the heart, in which we fall short daily (not loving God, neighbor, and self with all our heart, mind, soul, and strength), do not prove us to be unconverted persons. As a matter of fact, having <u>any</u> love for God, neighbor, and self, is proof that we <u>are</u> converted. In our natural state we hate God, we hate our neighbors, and we hate ourselves everyday and every hour on the hour. That is the nature of the fallen children of Satan, who is the master sinner who doesn't waste a solitary second in hesitating to do evil.

On the other hand, there is an area of activity, a persistent type of activity, which is demonstrative evidence that a person is <u>not</u> a Christian. You must examine yourself to see whether, in the area of what we usually call "gross sins," you persist. *He who is born of God* (I John 3:9) *does not sin*, in the sense of practicing these sins. If he does practice these sins, he is <u>not</u> born of God. Paul has a parallel to it in his fifth chapter of Galatians, where he lists the sins of the flesh as well as the fruits of the Spirit. The fruits of the Spirit prove that the Holy Spirit is living in you.

The <u>practice</u> of the fruits of the evil spirit in you is the proof that you are not born of God.

Paul mentions, as I say, about twenty evil fruits, and then ends with a statement "and such like," meaning that this is just a sample of gross sins. A person habitually practicing any of these demonstrates himself to be unconverted. Therefore he has no right whatever to assurance of eternal salvation.

Let me be specific in relating an episode that I have related publicly in preaching all around the country for a couple of years now. I have a friend who has been for years a practicing homosexual. This friend believes that the Bible is the Word of God and that the Bible condemns homosexuality and makes it very clear that practicing homosexuals will not inherit the kingdom of God. He also knows there is only one other place to inherit, and that is the kingdom of the devil in eternal hell. You don't have to persuade this homosexual that, if he does not conquer his practice, he will perish in hell.

The last time I saw my friend he said to me, "Dr. Gerstner, I've gotten it down to three times a week. Is there any hope for me now?" Though he had revelled grossly in this indescribable vice day in and day out, often many, many times in a given day, he is fighting against it, and has made what, for him, was remarkable progress. He had gotten it down to three times a week! Did that degree of success give him any right to consider himself no longer a homosexual under the wrath of God? I simply asked him, "Does practicing homosexuality three times a week define a homosexual or not?" The answer was as obvious to him as it was to me.

I once related this episode in a church. After the service, a number of the people came forward to the front to talk with me on various Christian matters. One thing unusual happened on that occasion. The counsellor of this church himself came forward. That is unusual because most ministers and counsellors do not come to these question periods, because they know they are meant for the regular members of the congregation and not for the staff. But this man came and actually monopolized the conversation. No one in the group resented it in the slightest. The reason they didn't resent it was the fact that this counsellor was obviously driven to ask questions. Everybody in that company was extremely interested in hearing the dialogue between us. They knew (as I at that time did not know, but I came to realize very quickly) that this man was counselling differently. They knew he would not doubt that that homosexual was no longer a homosexual. He undoubtedly would have given the man assurance that he was a sinner saved by grace. Being an orthodox man, the counsellor would have assured him that, once in a state of grace, he would remain in a state of grace. He would have counselled assurance of eternal salvation.

Naturally, he was greatly concerned with my difference on that matter, and so were the people. He asked me whether I was right in denying that that man was saved. "As you say, Dr. Gerstner, he is a believer in the Bible. He affirms Jesus Christ as Lord and Savior. He knows that homosexuality is a fatal sin. He is fighting against it, and making progress. How can you deny that he is a Christian saved by grace?"

I sympathized greatly with that counsellor for his concern. I even had a certain sympathy for the conclusion to which he felt himself driven. All I could say to him was this: "What can you call a man who practices homosexuality three times a week?" The homosexual couldn't come to any other conclusion than I, nor could the counsellor himself, ultimately. If one practices it once a month or once a year, wouldn't that define that person as a practicing homosexual?

It is a sadly amusing thing that, in our day, homosexual people constantly ask, "Why do you pick on the homosexuals all the time?" It is true that they are constantly being mentioned from pulpits in faithful churches. I answer people like that by saying that "We 'pick' on you because you brazenly maintain that you can be gay evangelicals. It is bad enough to sin; you glory in it! Furthermore, you are the only practicing gross sinners who actually insist on being ordained to the ministry of the Christian church. Adulterers, liars, thieves, addicts, and mafia members, don't usually call themselves saints and apply for ordination!

Once again, I repeat, if you examine yourself and find yourself practicing any vice, such as homosexuality, or promiscuity, or incest, or battering your wife, or battering your children, or robbing, or Sabbath-breaking, or not praying (there are people who say they are

Christians and yet don't pray), or living a secular life, you can't be in the kingdom of God. You name the sin. Paul names twenty of them. If you are living in sin, you are not in a state of salvation. You may have "assurance", but not of eternal life. You have assurance of eternal death (if you do not repent). *God is not mocked. Whatever a man sows, that he shall reap.*

KNOWING JESUS CHRIST
IS LOVING HIM IN THE HEART
AND OBEYING HIM IN THE LIFE.

Love Will Follow Me

Surely goodness and love will follow me all the days of my life, and I will dwell in the house of the Lord forever. (Psalm 23:6)

If *love will follow me all the days of my life*, I can't be anything but sure of eternal salvation, can I? David could not have been anything less, could he? You can't be anything other, can you? Must we not say, then, that Psalm 23 is an absolute assurance Psalm? Doesn't David even make assurance more sure? *...and I will dwell in the house of the Lord forever.*

But you remember that, on another occasion, David feared that God would take His Holy Spirit from him (Psalm 51:11). "How sure was he then?" you ask. Not very sure, I admit. So one time, a saint is sure of salvation and, on another occasion, is almost sure of judgment. Isn't that the way it is with all saints, all the time? On again, off again. He loves me, He loves me not.

Not quite. The David of Psalm 23 is a sure and serene David even in the valley of the

shadow and in the presence of his enemies.
It is the same man in Psalm 51, but under the
temporary chastening of his holy God against
Whom ("thee and thee only") he had sinned
most profanely. Though humbly praying, *Do
not cast me from your presence or take your
Holy Spirit from me,* David, sure that God
had not cast him away, begs that He restore
the joy of salvation and a "willing spirit"
(vss. 11-12). "Bloodguilt" is removed and the
king is able to win men, worship God, and
build Zion (vss.13-19).

Perhaps Psalm 51 is an even greater assurance Psalm than 23. In this Psalm, following
great sin, David's joy returns and his happy
fellowship is resumed, as God brings His
servant to deep repentance. David is sure
that God will never take His Holy Spirit away
from His chastened servant. When he asked
not to have the Holy Spirit taken from him,
he revealed that, in spite of his adultery-
murder, God had not cast him away. While
he was deeply humbled and hurt, he must
have known through his tears that his God
would never leave him. He would never repeat those crimes; but, even in God's anger,
the divine love and forgiveness shone
through. David, repentant David, knew God

would never leave him. He was sure of it.

Ah, but you say, could the time not come when David would not repent and would be destroyed by a God whose patience was gone (Ps.77)? Couldn't he be sure of that, too? If not sure, how could he be sure that time would <u>not</u> come? A certain author saw David seeking God through his many women. But David's God didn't see it that way. How long would He let His beloved shame His name? A harem, no less, for this beloved servant of the Lord who said, *from the beginning it was not so, but a man leaves his father and mother and cleaves to his wife alone?*

This is strange but, oddly, the Bathsheba sin was not that she was a multiple wife of David's, but the one wife of Uriah, a man who served the king faithfully, who betrayed him by taking his one ewe lamb. This must have been hard on David's assurance! Could he dwell in the same heaven with Uriah? Would God let him in such company? Could he imagine it, much less be sure of it?

I will dwell in the house of the Lord (with Uriah) *forever.* And with the little bastard child, and even with Bathsheba herself?

David may never had understood the Bathsheba love or lust, but he did know that he loved his God and couldn't stop believing that God loved him, too! Assurance based on sin? Surely not! But blessed assurance, Jesus is mine! Bathsheba didn't belong to him, but Jesus did. He may not have loved her, but he knew he loved Him. God may have taken his beloved child born in sin, but He could not leave His beloved child, David. David would go to heaven as surely as his illegitimate son did. The wonders of assurance are not in sin but through sin. Where sin abounded, grace yet more abounded.

Assurance has its quirks, but assurance it remains. The Lord will not let His beloved go, try as they sometimes may.

CAPTAIN CHRIST LEADS BEFORE
AND FOLLOWS BEHIND.

Man-made Insecurity

Catholicism had a human approach to the sacrament and the acceptance of the sacrament, by which faith came. Arminius actually had a human act of saving faith <u>before</u> the sacrament. So we see a progressive departure from the orthodox doctrine here. Rome teaches that man, in his sinfulness, brings himself to the sacrament, and then the sacrament (by God) does its own work of regenerating him. Wesleyan Arminianism takes one human step further. Man, without the sacrament, brings himself to faith in Christ, who then regenerates him.

<u>Wesleyan</u> Arminianism, however, has a special feature which makes its traditional opposition to assurance of salvation quite inconsistent. That is its doctrine of perfection. As we all know, John Wesley made that one of the tenets of his doctrinal emphasis. He was opposed to the Anglican Thirty-Nine Articles' doctrine of election, and also its doctrine of <u>im</u>perfection. Both of these departures Wesley promoted very vigorously. That is, he attacked the doctrine of election and the doctrine of imperfection, and promoted the

opposing doctrines strenuously. His very great friend, George Whitefield, not only differed with him on his deviations, but also reminded him that he was not being faithful to his Anglican vows. After all, Wesley was ordained affirming the Thirty-Nine Articles of the Church of England, which were Reformed, including the two doctrines which Wesley, later, so openly and knowingly opposed, in violation of his ordination vows.

The doctrine of perfection makes Wesley's opposition to assurance of salvation difficult. That is, if a person was filled with the love of God, why would he ever turn away from the love of God? If the Holy Spirit had taken dominion of his life, and he was perfect, how could he turn away? If he couldn't turn away, why would he not have assurance of eternal salvation? Wesley did not claim perfection for himself, but the doctrine of perfection which he taught is open to this inconsistency.

Romanism teaches the possibility not only of perfection, but "super-perfection" by means of works of super-erogation. Persons who had achieved perfection and super-perfection presumably didn't sin, and therefore would have assurance without any special revelation from heaven. But, apparently, neither Roman Catholic perfectionism nor Wesleyan perfectionism recognizes that that would rule out their opposition to assurance of eternal salvation.

Another interesting thing about John Wesley himself is that he was pretty sure of his salvation. He lived with great confidence. Though his doctrine allowed for a fall from grace even while in a state of perfection, nevertheless, many Wesleyans were confident of their salvation. Romans 8:16 was a favorite text (though, according to Arminian principles, that text gave no assurance that the Spirit's witness today would be the same tomorrow).

When you consider that the Roman Catholic church, the Greek Orthodox (which is essentially similar on this matter), the Lutheran church, and the fact that most of the conservative churches in the rest of Protestantism are now either expressly Arminian or at least Wesleyan Arminian, you can see that the overwhelming majority of professing Christendom is opposed to the great

Christian doctrine of assurance of eternal salvation.

ANY MAN-MADE SECURITY
IS SURE - TO FAIL.

Non-Assurance is Sin

As they sailed, He fell asleep. A squall came down on the lake, so that the boat was being swamped, and they were in great danger. The disciples went and woke Him, saying, "Master, Master, we're going to drown! "He got up and rebuked the wind and the raging waters. The storm subsided, and all was calm! "Where is your faith?"He asked His disciples. (Luke 8:22-25)

The disciples had Jesus in the boat with them, yet they were afraid their boat would sink in the storm and they would drown! They were not only not assured, but they were actually afraid - terrified. What sin! What gross sin and unbelief! Here was the divine Savior in the boat with them and, instead of sleeping calmly, they were in mortal fear of drowning! These couldn't possibly be disciples of Jesus, people who trusted their souls' everlasting happiness to Him who nevertheless were scared silly because of a little disturbance on a lake in Galilee. Impossible, you say. Not at all. They were as scared as if Jesus didn't exist at all while He was in the very same boat.

Yes, of course, He was asleep in that boat, to be sure. But what difference did that make? This was the Lord! As Peter said, "You know everything." They knew that while His body could become tired and sleep exhausted, this was also the Lord, the Lord of Israel who neither slumbers nor sleeps. The very fact that the Lord could permit His body to go to sleep ought to have added to the tranquility of His people, not to their anxiety and fear.

They should have felt sure. They should have had assurance of their salvation when they had Jesus with them in the same boat, so calm that He could sleep while the waves rose all about Him.

So, lacking assurance, they panicked. They lost faith. They gained terror. They doubted. They finally rebuked their Lord! To what depths of depravity a lack of sure trust can drive God's people to despair. They rebuked the Lord of glory, the Savior of their souls, who was about to shed His blood for them, of having no concern that they perished! What a stinging, though tender, rebuke they heard from the lips of an angry, aroused Lord.

If a person does not have assurance, he simply is not sure that his Lord will keep him as He promised. That person must be sure that the world, the flesh, and the devil are capable of doing what they are always trying to do - destroy his soul. He is sure of the devil when he is not sure of Christ. He has more confidence in Satan than in the Savior. The "strong man" who once held them captive is, for them, mightier than the Almighty. He has, for the moment, insulted the Most High. If this doubting Thomas continued this insulting lack of confidence in the Lord Jesus Christ, it would become apparent....

"Oh, you of little faith" would mean they were people of no faith. That was true of the Apostle, Judas Iscariot. And that would be true of you, you doubters of assurance of your salvation. You would have no faith in your professed Savior.

You see, you who so confidently teach against confidence, you unassured opponents of assurance, if this uncertainty were a true reflection of your heart (as of your erring mind), you would not be Christians at all.

After all, you do call yourselves believers. You consider yourselves saved by your faith. But faith is trust. Non-assurance is non-trust, non-faith, non-Christianity, non-salvation. We hope better things of you. Surely you aren't really unsure of Jesus Christ?

If you really are as insecure as you say you are...! But we trust that you only panicked; you forgot for an awful moment only that you are fellow-believers. You are true believers who only <u>say</u> you're not. <u>Reverse hypocrisy</u>. You really believe, though you say you don't.

We like to feel sure that you are sure, though you say, " 'tain't so!"

NON-ASSURANCE = NON-FAITH
AT THE MOMENT.

One for Whom Christ Died

Do not let what you eat cause the ruin of one for whom Christ died. (Romans 14:14)

Many suppose that this text is not only the end of a brother but it is also the end of any possible assurance of salvation. On the surface of it, it seems to say that a person for whom Christ died can actually be <u>destroyed</u> by the behavior of another Christian. If a person eats what, for him, is permissible but encourages a brother to eat, for whom it is a violation of conscience, another brother will be destroyed. And Christ died for that person, so the evil deed destroys Christ's work as well.

Surely if this is a brother for whom Christ died, and he is destroyed, it is undebatable that a Christian can indeed fall out of grace. If that is the correct interpretation of this passage, then I would certainly admit that assurance of salvation is unjustified by Holy Scripture. Let me try to show that however feasible that interpretation seems at first glance, it cannot stand under a second (not to mention a third or fourth) glance.

The <u>first</u> objection to that interpretation lies on the very surface of the text itself. The passage says that this is a brother for whom Jesus Christ died. Well, if Christ ever died for anyone, that person could never ever perish. Who can do anything against the Lord's Anointed? If God is for us, who can be against us? Christ's sacrifice is absolutely infinitely sufficient and utterly secures the salvation of anyone for whom it was made. To deny that would be to deny the gospel. That is the gospel: that God gave His Son to secure the salvation of those for whom He died. To entertain the opposite notion would be to say that Christ's death was futile. He died in vain. His sacrifice was not sufficient for all.

<u>Second</u>, since Christ could not have died for this brother and the brother he destroyed, what is the meaning of the text? One of two possibilities. Either the brother did not perish, or Christ did not die for him. Once again, as often, the Bible makes a person think. And remember, the Bible was given to the whole church, not just the clergy. So the Bible makes all of us think.

<u>Third</u>, the first theoretical possibility is that

the brother only <u>seems</u> to perish! The word
itself does not <u>demand</u> eternal perishing.
But the context does. This so-called brother is
represented as acting against his conscience,
and that is the same as to act against what he
considers to be the will of God. One who sets
himself (against his convictions) to defy the
will of God cannot be a Christian. The Christian says, "Thy will be done." He may sometimes misconstrue the will of God, but he
cannot resolutely disobey what he considers
to be the will of God.

It is also clear in the context that he is obeying the will of his fellow church members
against what he believes to be the will of
God. Thus, having their approval is more
important than having divine approval. He
has become a "men-pleaser" rather than a
true worshiper of God. This man is no mere
"weaker brother" as he seems to be, but an
idolator and wicked person. He is also a hypocrite only pretending to be a Christian
when, in fact, he is an idolator worshiping
men. Such a person's "ruin" spells hell.

<u>Fourth</u>, we are shut up to the only possible
interpretation. This person was truly ruined.
Therefore, Christ <u>could not</u> have died for

him. He <u>professed</u> to be one for whom Christ died; he was undoubtedly a member of the Roman congregation which considered him a true believer for whom Christ died.

If that seems a strained interpretation, let me remind you that the Bible frequently treats or refers to persons according to what they are thought to be, or what they think themselves to be, and not what they actually are. For example, take II Corinthians 13:5. There, the apostle says, *Examine yourselves to see whether you are in the faith. Test yourselves. Do you not realize that Christ Jesus is in you - unless, of course, you fail the test?* Paul is talking to Corinthian "Christians". That is, he is talking to those who thought of themselves as Christians and were thought by others to be Christians who may <u>not</u> have been Christians. He is telling the professed Christians to examine themselves to see if they are what they say they are. If not, they are not what they seem to be or think themselves to be. The apostle entertains the possibility that not everybody who professes the faith is indubitably what he seems to be. The conscience violator, tested by his behavior, is not a brother for whom Christ died. Paul is accommodating his language not to fact but to appearance, and describing a situation in which the person is <u>not what he seems to be - not one for whom Christ died</u>.

We have noticed under letter "J" that not all <u>are</u> Israel who are <u>in</u> Israel. Both groups were members in good standing in Israel, or in the church, as it were. But they were not all true believers. Not everyone who calls Christ "Lord" has Christ as Lord. They must, in the judgment of charity, be considered to be inwardly what they are outwardly, until there is evidence to the contrary.

I can go on with many, many other texts to the same effect. Enough has been cited to show that this Roman offender could not have been a true believer. No one for whom Christ actually died could be a practicing idolator, nor could he perish - unless the Son of God could die in vain.

Since this particular individual is described as one for whom Christ died and couldn't possibly be one for whom Christ actually died, one is forced to the conclusion (consistent with other passages in Scripture) that this person only <u>seemed to be</u> one for whom Christ died and was treated as such by the apostle and others as well. Since he only seemed to be such, he could actually not be such. Therefore, he could fall from his <u>professed</u> state of grace, not from a real state of grace. Obviously, that is not the same thing as saying that a person for whom Christ died, and who was in a state of grace, could indeed fall from that state of grace.

Therefore, we conclude that this passage superficially, at first glance, suggests that a person who actually was purchased by the blood of Christ perished. As a matter of fact, what it is saying is that a person who <u>appeared to be a believer</u> but was not, did, in reality, perish. Therefore, <u>it is no argument whatever</u> against the doctrine that a <u>true Christian</u> may have and ought to have an assurance of eternal salvation.

Footnote: Let me mention, incidentally, that the conscience-violator of Romans 14:14 <u>may have</u> been one for whom Christ died whose purchased salvation had <u>not yet</u> come to him. The point discussed above is that one for whom Christ died, <u>whose redemption had been applied to him</u> by the Holy Spirit's regeneration could never fall from grace and perish eternally. One may have been

"ruined" <u>at that time</u> who may later have
been saved and delivered from his idolatry,
thus proving that Christ, indeed, had died for
him.

BECAUSE NOMINAL CHRISTIANS CAN
PERISH DOES NOT PROVE THAT
TRUE CHRISTIANS CAN.

Pride Goes Before a Rise

Let him who boasts boast in the Lord.
(1 Corinthians 1:31)

The pride that goes before a fall excludes assurance and assurance excludes pride. That pride is pride of self. As the lady in Baltimore said to me after a sermon on sin, "You made me feel this big", reducing her thumb and fore-finger to the space of a half an inch. I, aghast, said, "That's too big!" That much self-esteem would take all the steam out of all virtue. Abandon <u>all</u> pride, all who would enter the kingdom of heaven.

But there is a pride that is as necessary for life as the other is fatal to it. God does not only require us to believe Him, to trust Him, to live for Him, and to die for Him but, most of all, to brag about Him.

You've got to be careful, however, not to brag about your bragging. When you boast about your boasting, you're boasting about you, not Him. You're proud of your pride in Him, not proud of Him.

If the devil can't stop your boasting in the God he hates, he'll trick you into boasting in your boasting about Him. "But," you ask, "doesn't the devil hate you as much as Him?" Of course not! There's so much more of Him to hate than measly you. You're hardly worth the time! God, says the prince of lies, is so perverse that He delights in your measly little boasting of Him. That's how small God is. So, if the devil can divert your little boasting of the all-great One, he'll come to see Him become enraged. How he loves to see God enraged because some insignificant thing stops bragging about Him! That comes close to satisfying his perfect hatred of the Holy One.

So, be careful lest your boasting in God becomes your boasting in your boasting, and you anger God and please the devil (if that were possible). At least, you make his misery a little less miserable as you share it with him.

PRIDE IN GOD IS LIFE - PRIDE IN SELF IS
DEATH, HERE AND HEREAFTER.

Question: Can You be an Unsure Christian?

...be all the more eager to make your calling and election sure. For if you do these things, you will never fall.... (II Peter 2:10)

A very fundamental question about assurance is whether a Christian can be without it and still be a Christian.

There is no question that a Christian <u>ought</u> to have assurance. There is the soundest basis for it. It would be abnormal not to have it. If a Christian does not have it, he must not understand Christian doctrine at that point, or be unsure whether he is a Christian.

Nevertheless, many, many persons claim to be unsure Christians; that is, Christians who are unsure of eternal salvation. Some who the church considers great heroes of the faith were devoid of it, at least at times. The Westminster Larger Catechism says it is "intermittent" (that does not mean that Christian assurance is intermittent, but that the person is not always sure that he or she is a Christian). Most seriously of all, some texts

of Scripture, such as the one above, seem to
teach it! With such considerations, and others that could be mentioned, it would seem
indubitable that "Can you be an unsure
Christian?" is not easy to answer.

Let us examine II Peter 2:10. <u>First</u>, it directs
Christians to be very eager to make their calling and election sure. That must mean make
<u>your</u> calling and election sure to yourself.
Divine calling and election are absolutely
sure. God does elect and He does call. There
is calling and there is election, to be sure.
Peter must mean, therefore, make sure <u>to</u>
<u>yourself</u> that you have been called and
elected.

Peter, no doubt, mentions calling first because, though it is second in order, it is first
in experience. **The persons who know they
have been called by God in time, know at
that time that they have been elected from
eternity**.

Some theologians conclude that, because the
apostle instructs Christians to make their
calling and election sure, they are not so at
the time he so commanded. If they already,
by virtue of being Christians, possessed their

calling and election surely, why would Peter tell them to make themselves sure? If so, assurance is not <u>essential</u> to being a Christian.

Is this a "good and necessary consequence" of Peter's teaching? The Christian must make salvation sure to himself. Therefore, it is not <u>necessarily</u> sure to himself!

I think this is a questionable deduction. The command to make sure would mean that it is a Christian's duty to be sure of one's eternal salvation. This assurance of calling and election <u>belongs</u> to professed Christians. They <u>must</u> possess it. It is a <u>duty</u>. Duties are not optional. No Christian does any duty perfectly, but he does it or he is not a Christian. *He who is born of God sins not.* (I John 3:9)

But a question arises here. A Christian must have assurance, yes, but it is imperfectly achieved. Is imperfect assurance not a contradiction in terms? How can one be <u>imperfectly sure</u>? If he is not altogether sure, he is not at all sure, is he?

True, imperfect assurance is <u>not</u> perfect assurance. But <u>imperfect faith</u> is not perfect faith. Nevertheless, we are perfectly justified.

The perfect justification of God, by the inter-
cession of Christ, perfects our imperfect faith.
Perfect pardon removes all the Christian's
imperfections of faith, hope, love, and assurance. In the eyes of God, our very imperfect
assurance would be, in the Beloved, nothing
less than perfect assurance. Every Christian,
however meager his assurance, possesses
perfect assurance!

So I Peter 2:10 means that every Christian has
imperfect assurance, perfect in Christ, and is
to perfect it more and more (as with all other
virtues). That must mean that assured
Christians are to "make their calling and
election" surer and surer to themselves.

Second, the next sentence confirms expressly
what the one just discussed implies. Peter
continues, after the exhortation to "make
sure," telling how to do so. *For if you do
these things, you will never fail.* Continuing
in the paths of virtue, the Christian is given
the assurance, *you will never fail.* If the
Christian is now on the straight and narrow
way, he will certainly arrive where it leads -
to heaven and eternal life.

Peter enumerated the various virtues at the

beginning of our paragraph:

> *For this very reason, make every effort to add to your faith goodness; and to goodness, knowledge; and to knowledge, self-control; and to self-control, perseverance; and to perseverance, godliness; and to godliness, brotherly kindness; and to brotherly kindness, love. For if you possess these qualities in increasing measure, they will keep you from being ineffective and unproductive in your knowledge of our Lord Jesus Christ. But if anyone does not have them, he is nearsighted and blind, and has forgotten that he has been cleansed from his sin.*

These are the "these things" which, if one does, he "will never fail." If one is doing these and knows he will never fail, what is that but an assured Christian? If he doesn't do them, it is because he is "blind" and no Christian, of which he can also be sure. He "has forgotten" (never knew) that he had <u>professedly</u> "been cleansed from his sin."

We have noticed more than once, in studying the ABC's, that if one knows the Bible, he is going to be an <u>assured person</u> - assured of eternal damnation <u>or</u> assured of eternal salvation. Usually one, by the grace of God, becomes assured of <u>salvation</u> only after first becoming assured of <u>damnation</u> in one's natural, fallen condition.

IF YOU DO "THESE THINGS", YOUR ELECTION IS SURE AND, IF YOUR ELECTION IS SURE, SO IS YOUR ETERNAL SALVATION.

Right-minded Versus High-Minded

Do not think of yourself more highly than you ought, but rather think of yourself with sober judgment, in accordance with the measure of faith God has given you.
(Romans 12:3)

It is an sad fact, noted above, that most of the churches which profess faith in Jesus Christ as Savior do not, and cannot, have assurance of Christ's salvation. Christ came to save His people, but a vast majority of those who claim His salvation live and die without any assurance of possessing His salvation.

The Roman Catholic church, for example, very definitely denies the possibility of assurance apart from a special revelation to some individuals. Lacking such special revelation, no true Christian (according to Romanism) can be assured that he will die in a state of grace and not go to hell. The Roman church is to be commended for consistency here. She does believe that fallen members of her own church can perish forever in unbelief. That includes her own priests as well as the Pope, for that matter. Unless a person has received this special communication from heaven, he and she must live out their days in uncertainty.

I am personally glad that Roman Catholics do <u>not</u> have assurance of salvation, since I do not believe that their doctrine is the Biblical doctrine on which true salvation is based. I consider it most unfortunate if Roman Catholics do think they have salvation even momentarily, not to mention assurance of everlasting salvation. Rome is consistently heretical. She is heretical on both points. She is heretical about the way of salvation. Consistent with that, she denies the possibility of the assurance of salvation and, therefore, is also heretical on that doctrine. At least her heresies hang together. She is consistently wrong. Rome is not like my inconsistent friend who professes the true way of salvation, and then goes on to deny the assurance that belongs to the true way of salvation. All this contemporary "evangelical" approval of Romanism, by Billy Graham and others, must mean that Rome has changed (which she denies), or that evangelicals have changed from the Reformation faith (which they deny)!

Another oddity about the Roman denial of
assurance of salvation is the source from
which it principally comes: the teaching of
Augustine. Among the claimed teachers of
the Roman church, Augustine is rated second only to Thomas Aquinas. As an aside, I
may say, if Rome had followed Augustine
she would have given up Romanism. However, Rome thinks that Augustine teaches
Roman doctrine. At this "assurance" point,
alas, he does. The great Augustine went
astray here. Augustine denied assurance and,
through his influence, the Roman Catholic
church denies it, too. I trust you see the irony
here. Augustine was a real Augustinian, not
a Roman Catholic at the heart of his theology. But, on assurance, he was Roman and
not his Augustinian self, though utterly
committed to the ultimate perseverance of
the saints .

The question is, why does Augustine deny
the possibility of assurance of salvation, since
he has a theology of the perseverance of the
saints on which it could and would normally
and properly rest? The strangest thing about
Augustine's denial of assurance is that it is
built on another oddly mistaken notion. In
my book Augustine, is probably the greatest

theological intelligence since the apostle Paul. His brilliance shines on just about every page he has ever written. But his reason for denying assurance of salvation seems to be an elementary mistake. This is it: assurance of salvation would, in Augustine's opinion, promote pride and presumption. For Augustine, pride was the original sin. It is the source, virtually, of all evil. Consequently he was very sensitive to anything proudful, anything arrogant, sensing immediately that it was utterly incompatible with the very spirit of the Christian religion. On that point, he was a true Augustinian, a true Reformed and Biblical mind.

Of course, if Augustine was right that assurance of salvation rested on and promoted pride and presumption, his conclusion would have been impeccable. Assurance, then, couldn't possibly be a Biblical doctrine. The Bible puts a premium on humility, insisting that those who abase themselves shall be exalted. It warns constantly against pride, insisting that those who lift themselves up shall be cast down. Pride was what lifted Lucifer up, and he was cast down to hell forever. Augustine will have nothing to do with anything that promotes pride.

We agree with Augustine completely here. No biblical doctrine, properly understood, can possibly promote pride in man. If anything can be shown clearly and indubitably and irrefutably to be the source of pride, we know it did not come from the Word of God. It couldn't be in the pages of Holy Writ.

But this is where Augustine goes strangely astray. Why would an assurance of salvation that rests entirely on the grace of God (He is the author of it, He is the finisher of it; the Alpha and Omega of salvation) puff up? We ourselves contribute absolutely nothing to it. We ourselves do not keep ourselves in a condition of grace for one moment. Our assurance is based absolutely and entirely on God and to no degree whatever on ourselves. We ask the great Augustine, how can pride get any legitimate entrance into the Christian heart on the basis of Christian theology? How could assurance of salvation, which rests entirely on God, give a Christian any room to boast about himself? How could he possibly answer Paul's statement "Boast not in thyself, let thy boasting be of the Lord." This kind of assurance of salvation leads to boasting, yes, but no boasting in one's self. It is boasting <u>in God alone</u> because

God alone is the source of the salvation on which our assurance actually rests. *It is because of Him that you are in Christ Jesus, who has become for us wisdom from God - that is, our righteousness, holiness, and redemption. Therefore, as it is written, 'Let him who boasts boast in the Lord.'* (I Corinthians 1:30-31).

It is not surprising that Lutheranism also became opposed to assurance of salvation. Luther had assurance of salvation, and seemed even to consider it essential to the Christian religion but, because of sacramental (*ex opere operato*) elements in his own theology, he did not recognize much later "Arminian" deviations. Lutheranism came to recognize the possibility of a fall from grace; and thus undermined the possibility of any genuine doctrine of assurance of salvation. It is obvious that once man becomes the controlling factor in salvation, salvation will become uncertain. Man, being sinfully fickle, is capable of departing from a given form of practice and belief. Thus, it becomes possible for him to turn away from the Christian faith. As long as <u>that</u> is a possibility, <u>assurance</u> of salvation is an impossibility. So we make the sad observation that the great

Lutheran church, spread all around the world, the faith of many millions, nevertheless, opposes assurance of salvation. No person holding logically to the official creed of Lutheranism, <u>The Book of Concord</u>, can, on those principles, have assurance of eternal salvation.

The whole Roman Catholic communion, the whole Lutheran communion, and many other Protestants, have <u>credally, not biblically, ruled out the possibility of assurance of eternal salvation</u>.

You may have read this meditation, looked again at the text, and wondered what the connection is. How does an excessive fear of pride show Augustine, Luther, Romanism, and Lutheranism, and other great traditions to be guilty of thinking too <u>highly</u> of themselves. It is because these friends think too highly of their contribution to assurance that they fear pride coming in. If they would remember that <u>Christ</u> is the Captain of our salvation, the Author and Finisher of our faith, the Alpha and Omega of our redemption, they would realize immediately and forever after that that it is easier for a camel to go through a needle's eye than for pride to claim the heart of the perfectly assured.

THE HIGHER OUR OPINION OF GOD,
THE LOWER OUR SELF-ESTEEM.

Security of Believers

If it is burned up, he will suffer loss; he himself will be saved, but only as one escaping through the flames. (I Corinthians 3:15)

There is nothing in Dispensationalism that is more strongly stressed than what they consider the doctrine of assurance of salvation. Of all the four points of Calvinism which they consider themselves to be maintaining, none is more stressed, more emphatically stressed, than the fifth point, the perseverance of the saints and the associated doctrine of assurance of salvation. I remember, for example, that Lewis Sperry Chafer and John Walvord, in their volume Bible Doctrines, give no less than fifty texts which they believe teach the perseverance of the saints and the associated doctrine of assurance of salvation. But, I'm afraid, as we look at the teaching of Dispensationalism, we find that, instead of being the strongest supporters of the doctrine of assurance, they are actually underminers of the doctrine.

Dispensationalists' understanding of the fifth point of Calvinism, perseverance of the

saints, is essentially <u>antinomian</u> in character.
They maintain that, once a person professes
faith in Jesus Christ, he is going to be in Jesus
Christ forever. He will never, no matter how
he lives, cease to be saved in Christ. He is
incapable of falling out of once-professed
faith.

The reason for their confidence is that they
assume that profession of faith is saving
faith. Even today, after a very strong debate
on the subject precipitated by John Mac-
Arthur's <u>The Gospel According to Jesus</u>, the
Dispensationalists are still hanging in there
with the doctrine of assurance of the salvific
character of their faith, even though that
faith may not be followed by good works.
They believe that good works <u>should</u> be the
product of that faith. They urge fellow Christians to do good and heap up a great reward
in the world to come, but they cannot be per-
suaded that the <u>profession</u> of faith in Christ,
the virgin-born, divine Son of God could be
anything other than saving.

Does I Corinthians 3:15 not confirm the
dispensationalists? <u>First</u>, let us consider the
<u>Ryrie Study Bible</u>'s interpretation of this
passage: (NASB)

2. Rewards will be lost, 3:10-4:5

10 According to the grace of God which
was given to me, as a wise master
builder, I laid a foundation, and
another is building upon it. But let each
man be careful how he builds upon it.
11 For no man can lay a foundation
other than the one which is laid,
which is Jesus Christ.
12 Now if any man builds upon the
foundation with gold, silver, precious
stones, wood, hay, straw,
13 each man's work will become evi-
dent; for the day will show it, because
it is to be revealed with fire; and the
fire itself will test the quality of each
man's work.
14 If any man's work which he has
built upon it remains, he shall receive a
reward.
15 If any man's work is burned up, he
shall suffer loss; but he himself shall
be saved, yet so as through fire.

This is the comment on 3:10-15 as a whole:
"This passage refers to the judgment seat of
Christ (cf. II Corinthians 5:10). The works
discussed here have nothing to do with earning or losing salvation. The rewards (or loss
of them) pertain only to Christians."

One never says that works "have nothing to

do with earning or losing salvation." They
<u>always</u> prove the presence or absence of sal-
vation. *Faith without works is dead* (James
2:26), or, as we have seen, doing good works
proves you will arrive at your salvation goal.

Furthermore, the Ryrie Bible contradicts the
Bible at another point. It interprets "wood,"
(and presumably "hay and straw" as well) as
works "which are ultimately worthless."
The man who does nothing but worthless
works will still be saved. This is the fatal
Antinomianism endemic to Dispensationalism. Legalism also comes in via that same
verse 12, because "gold" (and presumably
"silver, precious stones" as well) is "valu-
able," and will <u>merit</u> and receive "reward" at
the believer's judgment. However, the
"works" of Christians are so defiled by remaining corruptions that, though they will
receive "rewards," they <u>never earn</u> them.
"Rewards" are themselves <u>gracious</u>, in relation to, but not deserved by, the utterly
<u>imperfect</u> works of the best Christians.

Christian salvation, however, is <u>merited</u>
by works and no other way. Christ's <u>passive
obedience</u> earned the cancellation of the
believer's guilt, and His <u>active obedience</u>

purchased the believer's righteousness. They are "free" to the believer in the sense that <u>he</u> could do no "works" worthy of anything but damnation. But it is <u>the meritorious work of Christ, imputed</u> to the believer, that <u>purchases</u> his salvation by the vicarious satisfaction of Christ for his sins. It is because the believer does have Christ's righteousness, and only for that reason, that he is acceptable to God. He is made "<u>acceptable in the Beloved</u>."

On the other hand, works have everything to do with man's damnation. He, himself, merits condemnation because of the heinousness of his sins, every one of which earns eternal hell.

Dispensationalism is consistently wrong, but the error we notice here is its fatal perversion of "security" or assurance. It makes security to rest on no foundation. The very foundation mentioned in I Corinthians 3:11 is Jesus Christ. But no one is resting on Christ who does nothing but "worthless" works. Easy-believism denies that the person is in Christ, because Christ insists, *If you love me, keep My commandments.* The Dispensationalist should realize that, as James said, *faith without works is dead,* and that faith with nothing but "worthless" works of "wood, hay, straw" (interpreted as non-works) describes such persons who cannot possibly be resting on Christ as their foundation. The dispensationalists should be sure that such persons, being devoid of works, cannot be saved by fire, but will be damned by fire.

If the reader asks what I Corinthians 3:15 <u>does</u> mean by saying that the "wood, hay, straw" person *will suffer loss; yet he himself shall be saved yet as through fire*, let us see. It <u>cannot</u> mean what <u>The Ryrie Study Bible</u> teaches (as shown above). What it would seem to be saying is that true Christians have differing degrees of fruitfulness (some thirty-fold, some sixty-fold; some a hundred-fold) ranging from straw to gold. Some will have great reward and some very little. "Rewards," though they do not rest on merit (which no Christian has of himself), are graciously distributed <u>in relation to works</u> so that even a cup of cold water given in Christ's name will have everlasting blessing (Matthew 10:42) Suffering "loss" would probably refer to Christians who do not redeem the time well in this world by laying up great treasure in heaven for an abundant entrance into glory. Their opportunity is now gone forever.

EVEN WEAK SAINTS ARE SECURE BY THE
BLOOD OF CHRIST, THOUGH HANGING
ON BY THE SKIN OF THEIR TEETH.

P.S. The above discussion is based on the interpretation of I Corinthians 3:10-15 as refer-
ring to the testing of a professed Christian's
state in relation to his works. This is a com-
mon, and possible, interpretation. The other
interpretation, which I think more likely, is
the testing of ministers (such as Paul and
Apollos with reference to their service in
building up congregations. Whichever general interpretation is correct, Dispensationalism tends, always, like Dr. Ryrie, to use 3:15
as meaning that individual Christians may
be saved without works, or with "useless
works". This dreadful interpretation has the
Bible teaching another gospel called
"Antinomianism," and basing assurance in it
(as shown in the critique above).

Taking Out of Christ's Hand is Impossible

I give them eternal life, and they shall never perish; no one can snatch them out of My hand. My Father, who has given them to Me, is greater than all; no one can snatch them out of My Father's hand. I and the Father are one. (John 10:28-29)

One would think desperate Christians, knowing how weak and prone to wander they are, would grasp eagerly at this text. What a grand assurance to know that Christ Himself will hold us tightly forever! But here again we stare at the incredible fact that most Christians will not take assurance when it is given to them by the hand of Christ. They will not go to Him unless He guarantees that they can go from Him.

This strongest of assurance texts seems to have an Arminian evangelical escape hatch. True, Arminians say, no one other than I can take me out of Christ's almighty hands. He invites me to come to Him and stay with Him. If I am able to come, I must be able not to come. Or, if I do come, I must be able not to stay. I admit that not to come or stay would be foolish. Not to accept this invitation in the first place is foolish, and it is more foolish to leave Him in the second place. But that possibility is what Christ is dealing with when He takes on people like us. We are people who can come to Him and go from Him. If we can't come or go, we are simply not true human beings as He made us.

We have dealt with this kind of Arminian opposition to assurance of salvation under chapter "F." That was dealt with there in rather general terms. Here, the point is greatly intensified by the Arminian's insisting that their sheer power of choice is mightier than the choice of Jesus Christ. Their wills are more powerful than Christ's "hand." I, for one, would be terrified if that were so:

> Prone to wander, Lord, I feel it;
> Prone to leave the God I love.

Here again is a twisting of Scripture. Christ says that <u>no one</u> can snatch them out of His hand. The Christian is among the "no one"s! Christ does not say, "No one but the person himself can snatch them out of My hand."

The Arminian will say that this is implied. Christ talks about "snatching them." People don't snatch themselves. They are snatched; presumably by someone else. The devil is always trying to snatch back those Christ snatched from his mighty grasp. And if Satan can't snatch them out of Christ's hand, no other individual could do it because Christ has no more powerful enemy.

HERE IS THE ASSURANCE OF ASSURANCE,
CHRISTIAN:YOU CAN'T TAKE YOUR-
SELF OUT OF CHRIST'S HANDS
EVEN IF YOU TRIED!

Uncertain, Trembling Assurance

...continue to work out your salvation with fear and trembling; for it is God who works in you to will and to act according to His good purpose. (Philippians 2:12-13)

Opponents of assurance appeal to Philippians 2:12-13. How can a person who is in a state of <u>assured</u> grace, as the people here are described in this passage, still work out their own salvation with <u>fear and trembling</u>? Where does the fear and trembling come in for people who are absolutely sure that they will never fall from grace but will arrive at their heavenly destination? It would seem to us, they say, that if a person works out his salvation with fear and trembling, he is something less than secure. That language suggests insecurity, uncertainty, not tranquility. "Why would a person tremble if, as you keep saying, God is for us and nobody can be against us? If no one can take us out of Christ's hands, why the anxiety? We folk who don't believe in assurance of salvation seem to have more confidence and joy in our uncertain salvation than you do in your certain salvation."

Admittedly, that is a good question. Anxiety and security are mutually exclusive concepts. You can't be serenely sure of your arriving at your heavenly destination and at the same time, trembling for fear you will not. This serenity gospel doesn't <u>seem</u> too serene.

The context certainly seems to say that the Christian is working out his salvation - his eternal salvation. But the way in which one travels the assured road could cause fear and trembling along the way. That is to say, I could be sure of my salvation, and yet tremble and be afraid of the way I am thinking and living.

For example, someone is right now criticizing my doctrine here. Since I am not infallible, and since my opponent is capable of understanding truth better than I, it is quite possible that he is right and I am wrong. That fact, not the assurance doctrine, could scare me. Isaiah, who certainly had no question about his own salvation, was trembling at the Word of God (Isaiah 66:2). Even though he was a prophet, he could misunderstand or misinterpret the Word of God, even when he was the vehicle for its infallible recording. People who were the source of truth were not always capable of understanding the truth which came to them by God. They could relay it as God gave it. Nothing else would be possible if <u>God</u> was communicating His revelation through them. They would be rendered free of any error whatever in the inscripturation of this Word. However, all of that does not guarantee that they would be free of error in understanding. Just as the people to whom the Word was communicated could misinterpret it, so the man by whom it was communicated could not misstate it, but could misinterpret it. So there would be room even for an inspired prophet to tremble. There would be even more room for an uninspired prophet to tremble. We would not be trembling about the doctrine of assurance of salvation, but we could be trembling about our understanding it or our practice, and whether that entitles us to what the Bible teaches on assurance of salvation. Is that not possible?

Let me take this a step further, and ask it with respect to Paul himself, as we have just considered it with respect to Isaiah. Granted that when Paul by divine inspiration said that we should work our salvation with fear and trembling, was it not true that Paul was working out his salvation with fear and trembling? He had assurance. He knew that He whom he had believed would carry him through to the day of redemption. He declared in the end of his life, *I have fought a good fight, I have finished the course, I have kept the faith, henceforth is laid up for me a crown of righteousness.*

As a matter of fact, must we not say that Paul did work out his own salvation with fear and trembling, because he was a Christian? He was not perfect. He never claimed that he was without sin. Paul commanded the Corinthian Christians to examine themselves, not to see whether the doctrine of the Bible was true, but to see whether they were true believers, or whether examination could show that they were not.

Shall I put it this way? Every Christian who is assured of salvation <u>is assured of salvation if, indeed, he is a Christian</u>. At the same time, he knows that, if he is not a Christian, he has no justifiable assurance of salvation. That is enough to make anyone tremble as he examines himself. Understanding a doctrine is by no means the same as standing under that doctrine. Grasping something with the mind, is not the same thing as embracing it with the heart. Though you can't embrace with the heart what you don't understand with your mind, you can understand with your mind what you don't embrace with the heart.

Consequently, a person who is orthodox in his thinking could tremble even more because he realizes so well, that though orthodoxy is essential to salvation, orthopraxy of the heart and life are essential to orthodoxy. Since he does have an orthodoxy of the mind, he knows that doesn't guarantee that he has the right to the assurance of salvation. So the more sound a person is in doctrine, the more likely he is to work out his salvation with fear and trembling. He knows what indicates a person is a secure believer and what does not indicate it, and what even proves the opposite.

Errorists have a tendency to be confident in their errors, and aren't much afraid because they have superficial security. That does not belong to people who think soundly. Knowledge puffs up. It does not, by itself, sanctify. Though we cannot have salvation without knowledge, we can have knowledge without salvation; as our Lord prayed, *This is life eternal, that they know Thee, the only true God, and Jesus Christ whom Thou hast sent.* Francis Schaeffer once said that "knowing God" is <u>at least</u> rational knowledge, but it is <u>more</u> than rational knowledge. The question you and I (who have a rational knowledge of the way of salvation) must ask ourselves is, do we know Him who is the way of salvation <u>salvifically</u>? There is plenty of room there for fear and trembling.

I know at that point that an individual of the other persuasion will immediately close in and say "Look, if that is the case, how can you ever have assurance of salvation? How can you ever have anything but fear and trembling?"

I answer that directly by saying that fear and trembling do not exclude or reject assurance even at the moment that you are examining yourself. However, having examined yourself with fear and trembling, you can confirm that you do have a sound reason for being confident.

You re-examine the arguments from the

other side of the aisle, reassure yourself that they do not stand up under analysis, and that the attacks on you are not well grounded. The sound arguments you have for this doctrine are accompanied by a genuine acceptance of assurance. The objector is assuming that a careful self-examination will render a negative verdict. Of course it may. It may also render a positive verdict. After re-examining oneself he can be more sure than ever that he is in a state of grace from which the Bible makes it perfectly clear that he can never ever fall.

UNCERTAIN CERTAINTY IS
A CONTRADICTION, BUT
TREMBLING CERTAINTY IS NOT.

Vines Dying on the Branch?

I am the true vine and my Father is the gardener. He cuts off every branch in me that bears no fruit, while every branch that does bear fruit he trims clean so that it will be even more fruitful. You are already clean because of the word I have spoken to you. Remain in me, and I will remain in you. No branch can bear fruit by itself; it must remain in the vine. Neither can you bear fruit unless you remain in me.

I am the vine; you are the branches. If a man remains in me and I in him, he will bear much fruit; apart from me you can do nothing. <u>If anyone does not remain in me, he is like a branch that is thrown away and withers; such branches are picked up, thrown into the fire and burned</u>. If you remain in me and my words remain in you, ask whatever you wish, and it will be given you. This is to my Father's glory, that you bear much fruit, showing yourselves to be my disciples. (John 15:1-8 NIV)

I once addressed a Congregational Seminary on "perseverance." I know that the historic Congregational church was Reformed and cherished that doctrine. Since this was an annual lectureship, all the officials of the little denomination were present. In the midst of my lecture, the top official rose to correct my exposition and indignantly rebuke me for attacking their cherished Arminian doctrine of a possible non-persevering saint. Before he sat down, he reminded me that, furthermore, Christ clearly taught their doctrine as shown in John 15!

I did apologize for a certain breach of etiquette on my part, explaining that, since the denomination was "Congregational," I assumed that it was Reformed. I also assumed that no denomination would invite me to denounce what they maintained to be true unless it was to be a debate. Having apologized for the misunderstanding, I assured the official and the audience that I made no apology for the doctrine of perseverance, and I explained John 15:1-8 as I am about to explain it to you, my readers, now.

I admit at the outset that this text does <u>seem</u> to be "Arminian." At first glance here, the Lord does seem vividly to teach a possible fall from grace of true Christians. And if Jesus Christ taught once anywhere a possible fall from grace, the doctrine of perseverance and assurance is profound heresy! That, any true Christian will always admit.

But Christ and the Word of God do not anywhere teach a possible fall of a true saint. So what is the explanation of John 15:1-8?

First, John 15:1-8 is part of an analogy. It is drawing a parallel between Christ as a vine and His true believers as human branches. They are in Him as a branch is in a vine. They receive their life from Him and bear fruit by His life surging through them. Because branches never have perfect union with their vines and need pruning, so the Father is the pruner of these branches.

Some branches do die on the vine and so, it would seem, true Christians can be separated from the Vine, die, be cut off and thrown into hell fire. But Christ had already, in non-allegorical but literal language, said that no one can take His disciples out of His hand. Also, having loved His own, He loved them to the end of His life. He promised to have a residence in heaven waiting for them when they died, John 14:2. And so goes all the rest of His teaching, as well as that of the entire

Bible. So we <u>know</u> that every part of this <u>allegory</u> is not to be construed as Christ's deliberate teaching.

<u>Second</u>, if anyone insists on making something doctrinal of John 15:6, it would have to be what we have shown in other of our ABC's, especially chapter "D." There are "visible" Christians who are not true Christians. They appear to be in Christ, but are not in reality. So the time comes when their pretense becomes evident to the church, and they are excommunicated or, at the Day of Judgment, it is seen by the whole world, and they go into the fires of endless punishment (Matthew 25:46).

<u>Third</u>, the easy mis-interpretation of this verse is a deliberate, divine warning that even Bible-believing readers of God's Word must not only look, but tremble, before they leap. It is easy to wrest Scripture to one's destruction if he does not tremble lest he err. But it is impossible for tremblers to misunderstand the doctrine (which is one and unified). God never contradicts Himself. Liberals who do not acknowledge the Bible to be the Word of God, which it is, can find whatever they wish in it and brazenly tell the

world it can get whatever it wants out of the
Bible. They will find out otherwise on the
Day of Judgment if they do not learn to trem-
ble before that time.

<u>Fourth</u>, one cannot doubt that God intends
these easily-misunderstood portions to force
people to be very careful. With due care, they
can be understood as perfectly harmonious
with the rest of Scripture. With careless
study, or vested interests, or over-confidence,
or any number of non-trembling hermeneu-
tics, one can go astray.

<u>Fifth</u>, the irony of this erroneous interpreta-
tion is that it misses altogether the most vital
truth which the Parable of the Vine indubitably does teach. Christ is the Christian's
life. Paul says that for him to live is Christ,
and Christ gives Paul, and all other believers,
a dynamic picture of this wonderful verity in
the divine Vine. Christ redeems sinners who
come alive and stay alive because of Christ in
them. If they are in <u>this</u> Vine, they will never
become dead branches. *He who believes in
Me shall never die.* If Christ will not let a
Christian be taken out of His hand, what can
that mean but that he will not let a branch be
taken out of its divine Vine?

Sixth, apparently our Lord throws this allusion to dead branches in to make His people think. "Consider," "think", "meditate", "ponder", "reflect", "remember" are a refrain throughout Scripture. We are commanded to love God with all our minds. He who believes does not make haste. Snap judgments are hermeneutical catastrophes.

I press on toward the goal to win the prize for which God has called me heavenward in Christ Jesus. All of us who are mature should take such a view of things. And if on some point you think differently, that too God will make clear to you. Only let us live up to what we have already attained. (Philippians 3:14-16)

"FOR ME TO LIVE IS CHRIST" -
THE CHRISTIAN LIFE IS THE
CHRIST-LIFE WHICH CANNOT DIE.

Warning to Assured Believers!

So be on your guard! Remember that for three years I never stopped warning each of you day and night with tears. (Acts 20:31)

The Bible abounds with warnings to Christians about turning away from Christ, falling off from faith. The opponents of assurance of salvation argue that, if it is possible for a person to fall from grace, certainly he can't have assurance of eternal salvation. And warnings about falling away prove that very possibility. I agree to this, that if warning Christians about falling from grace proves the possibility of falling from grace, assurance of eternal life is a false doctrine.

Where does the threatening Bible say that true Christians can fall from grace? I maintain that there is not a single text in Scripture anywhere that says that a regenerate Christian person can become unregenerate. I, therefore, challenge the objector to give me one such text. If he can, I will grant his point.

The objector is delighted and says, "I will show you dozens of texts. So if one will convince you of your error, I will deluge you with proofs that you are teaching false doctrine." Dozens will not be necessary, I say. One will suffice.

The objector cites the text above, Acts 20:31, *So be on your guard! Remember that for three years I never stopped warning each of you day and night with tears!* That text surely leaves no doubt whatever that the Apostle Paul warned everyone in the church constantly with tears.

No one questions that the people of God are constantly warned. Nor is it doubted that warnings pertain to perishing. In the verses preceding this text, Paul had already foretold the Ephesian elders that *after I leave, savage wolves will come in among you and will not spare the flock. Even from your own number, men will arise and distort the truth in order to draw away disciples after them.* Distorting truth, drawing visible saints away from the church, and making them disciples of these "savage wolves" surely spells their eternal doom. All of this happened shortly after, and in spite of, Paul's three years of warning the churches.

But is there any instance given or predicted of one <u>true</u> believer who was drawn away by distorted truth to leave Christ and follow "savage wolves?" That, Paul never reports or predicts.

The Bible does teach that there will always be tares among the wheat, whom the church must not even attempt to remove, but who are quite capable of going out from the church because they are not of the church. They are the only ones the "savage wolves" could draw away to death. This is not to deny that true sheep can be hurt because of careless shepherds or careless sheep! But the Great Shepherd will never let one of His own be destroyed. And a million warnings of wolves who always surround and threaten them and lead them to move with great care do not prove that a solitary one of them will ever perish. But the Great Shepherd does warn His sheep that they can be PAINFULLY HURT, THOUGH NEVER KILLED.

ABSOLUTE ASSURANCE OF SAFE ARRIVAL
DOES NOT MEAN "NO PERIL EN ROUTE."

(E)**X**horting Assured Believers to Persevere

So do not throw away your confidence; it will be richly rewarded. You need to persevere so that when you have done the will of God, you will receive what he has promised. For in just a very little while, "He who is coming will come and will not delay. But my righteous one will live by faith. And if he shrinks back, I will not be pleased with him." But we are not of those who shrink back and are destroyed, but of those who believe and are saved. (Hebrews 12:35-39)

Here, the inspired writer exhorts professed believers, *do not throw away your confidence....* He also finds it necessary to remind them that they *need to persevere,* and *only when you have done the will of God* will you *receive what he* (God) *has promised.* Moreover, *the righteous will live by* (continued) *faith.* Warningly, our author says that if the professed believer *shrinks back,* God *will not be pleased with him.* The conclusion is, *but we are not of those who shrink back and are destroyed, but of those who believe and are saved.*

Here we have: (1) An exhorting of the believer not to "throw away your confidence," which does not say that he will - or even can. We saw in chapter "B" that, though Paul's beating his body lest he be cast away did not imply that he could or would cease and be cast away. An exhortation to a believer not to throw away his confidence (but, rather, to hold on to it) <u>does not imply that he would or could throw assurance away</u>, but only that he should hold on to it, which is to urge him to do his duty, PERIOD.

(2) Likewise, urging them to the necessity of persevering carries no notion that they may not. In Philippians 2:12-13, we are told why a believer will continue to work out his salvation (namely, because God is at work in him so to do). In this passage, the believer is told to persevere though it is not added (as it could have been) "because God is working in you to persevere."

I am not begging the question here by suggesting that that was implied, but am only saying that it <u>could have been</u>. The point is simply that an exhortation to a person to persevere does not <u>necessarily</u> imply that he must be morally able not to do so. That would have to be true if the objection were to be valid.

(3) Again, the fact that only when the will of God has been done will the doer receive God's promises carries no implication that a person cannot now be sure that he will do the will of God and receive the promise. All that is implied is that perseverance is necessary - not that a true Christian can <u>not</u> endure to the end. The same can be said about the necessity of one continuing in faith to continue to "live."

(4) If the believer draws back, God will have no pleasure in him just as, if Paul stopped self-discipline, he would perish, and if Christ denied He knew God, He would be a liar. The text does not say or imply that a true believer <u>can</u> draw back fatally, but only what would happen IF he did draw back.

(5) I have shown that all these negative exhortations (don't throw away your confidence, don't cease to persevere, don't stop walking in faith, and don't fail to do your duty if you would receive the promises) in no way imply that true Christians can <u>do so</u> simply because they are exhorted <u>not to do</u>

<u>so</u>!

This last statement is a positive assertion that "we (who are true believers like the inspired writer) are not of those who shrink back and are destroyed, but of those who believe and are saved." Once again, true believers or disciples are, by definition, those who abide, continue in, walk in, go in, and work out their salvation; who, in a word, are "those who believe and are saved." They are not *those who shrink back and are destroyed....*

So again, if you are a disciple, you are a continuing-to-the-end disciple. There are no other varieties. In the visible church, there are two kinds: those who can draw back and those who cannot. Only the latter are true disciples of Jesus Christ.

THE BIBLE EXHORTS TO THE INEVITABLE.

Yellow Christians

Whoever disowns Me before men, I will disown him before My Father in heaven.
(Matthew 10:33)

The story is told of a man who was to be burned alive for his witness to Jesus Christ. He was afraid his fear would overcome his faith. Hoping to prepare himself for the ordeal, he put his finger in a candle flame and couldn't hold it there but a few seconds. He was afraid he would deny Christ when he faced a raging furnace the next day. But when the time came, he perished bravely as a witness to the One who had died for him.

Suppose he hadn't? Would he later have died eternally in the flames of hell? Our text seems to say he would. To underline this stern doctrine, Jesus commands: *If you deny Me before men, I will deny you before My Father.* Christ is warning us that if we do not confess Him in any circumstances whatever, He will not confess us before His Father in heaven. The Apostle Peter buckled and lied before the accusing finger of a serving maid. Even after Pentecost, he had denied Christ at

Antioch because he feared criticism from Judaizers. But he died - if tradition be accurate - crucified head down, not feeling worthy even to die in the same position as his Lord.

Could Peter, clearly a saint however fainthearted and even "yellow" he might have been, have had assurance of his eternal salvation when he feared those who could only destroy the body?

Peter's own epistle shows that he was fully assured. However terrified of torture and death he may have been, he knew Christ would not let him go and, therefore, he would never let Christ go. He could be sure of that. However totally unsure of himself he may have continued right through his martyr's death, he was sure of his Lord. After all, all true assurance is not only in a "love that will not let us go," but in spite of the weakness of the Christian's love which, of itself alone, would let Christ go at the first approach of danger.

As a matter, there may be more danger to assurance in being lion-hearted than being yellow. No yellow person is going to be tempted to self-pride and glory. A naturally brave person may be relying confidently <u>in himself</u>, a perfect ground for non-assurance.

A natural Christian coward will flee to the Rock that is greater than he, and there *the righteous are as bold as a lion.* (Proverbs 28:1)

YELLOW IS NOT TRUE-BLUE.

Zero to Zenith

If you talk assuredly of your possession of eternal life, the overwhelming majority of people who hear you will be tempted to think you have pride.

Does that mean you ought not to tell your assurance to other people? No, but you must be doubly careful to make it very clear to people that you have no <u>self</u>-confidence. You are not sure of yourself, even of your <u>love</u> for Jesus Christ! <u>Left to yourself</u>, you would be incapable of <u>not</u> falling away. Peter loved Jesus and really thought that he would follow Him to death. Even when Christ told him that the devil desired to sift him like wheat, and that before the rooster crowed he would deny Christ three times, Peter didn't believe it. He loved Jesus so much that he could not imagine his denying Him.

Peter was a fool, not a hypocrite. He really thought his love was that great that he would be incapable of denying Jesus Christ. There was that pride of which Augustine was so afraid.

Peter was sure of his love for Christ. He had a love for Christ, but he overestimated it. He thought more highly of himself (his love) than he ought. He, Simon Peter, thought himself incapable of denying his Lord. He erred in his self-esteem. He sinned. He repented later, but he did sin.

Peter did not sin as a result of assurance of salvation. He sinned in having the wrong basis for his assurance on that occasion. His failure should have sobered him up. As a matter of fact, it did. Afterward, he did as his Lord had said, *when you have turned back, strengthen your brothers* (Luke 22:32).

Now Peter strengthens everyone of us. He says to us, "loving Jesus Christ (truly) does not mean we do not have any remaining love for the world, the flesh, and the devil. We must be on our guard at all times. Be confident in Christ. His words, *I have prayed for you that your faith not fail,* is the only reason I did not perish in the hands of Satan that terrible night. I am still sure and boasting, but not in Simon Peter, only in my Lord Jesus Christ."

That is the voice of assurance of life eternal.

May we all, my readers, have it. And may we tell that story to the nations, but in a way that Jesus Christ will be glorified.

"There" (as we contemplate hell) "<u>but for</u> the grace of God go I."

"There" (as we contemplate heaven) "<u>because of</u> the grace of God, go I."

FROM ZERO (ME) TO ZENITH (GOD).

SOLI DEO GLORIA!